MAN IS
THE ONLY ANIMAL
THAT BLUSHES...
OR NEEDS TO

THE WISDOM OF
MARK TWAIN

MAN IS
THE ONLY ANIMAL
THAT BLUSHES...
OR NEEDS TO

THE WISDOM OF
MARK TWAIN

Selected by: Michael Joseph

STANYAN BOOKS

RANDOM HOUSE

A Stanyan book
Published by Stanyan Books,
8721 Sunset Blvd., Suite C
Los Angeles, California 90069,
and by Random House, Inc.
201 E. 50th Street,
New York, N.Y. 10022

Designed by Hy Fujita

Printed in U.S.A.

All that I care to know is that a man is a human being. That's enough for me; he can't be any worse.

**Kindness is a language which the deaf
can hear and the blind can read.**

Wrinkles should merely indicate where
smiles have been.

Grief can take care of itself; but to get the
full value of joy, you must have somebody
to divide it with.

Tobacco is an Indian weed. Wahoo!

Man is the only animal that blushes —
or needs to.

There are times when one would like to
hang the whole human race, and
finish the farce.

**If you pick up a starving dog and make him
prosperous, he will not bite you.
This is the principal difference between
a man and a dog.**

. . . until man shall develop into something
really fine and high — some billions of
years hence, say.

Adam and Eve had many advantages, but the principal one was that they escaped teething.

We like a man to come right out and say what he thinks — if we agree with him.

We ought never to do wrong when people are looking.

Few things are harder to put up with than the annoyance of a good example.

I have been complimented many times and they always embarrass me; I always feel they have not said enough.

Let us endeavor so to live that when we come to die even the undertaker will be sorry.

There are two times in a man's life when he should speculate; when he can't afford it, and when he can.

Fleas can be taught nearly everything
that a Congressman can.

In Boston they ask, How much does he know?
In New York, how much is he worth?
In Philadelphia, Who were his parents?

In the South the war is what A.D. is
elsewhere; they date from it.

Everything human is pathetic. The secret source of Humor itself is not joy but sorrow.

Thunder is good, thunder is impressive, but it is lightning that does the work.

It is curious that physical courage should be so common in the world, and moral courage so rare.

Training is everything. The peach was once a bitter almond; cauliflower is nothing but cabbage with a college education.

Familiarity breeds contempt — and children.

To be a writer, one must observe three
rules: (1) write, (2) write, and (3) write.

**My books are water; those of the great
geniuses are wine — everybody drinks water.**

As to the adjective, when in doubt,
strike it out.

Write without pay until somebody offers
pay; if nobody offers within three years,
sawing wood is what you were intended for.

**A classic is something that everybody
wants to have read and nobody wants to read.**

I make it a point never to smoke more than
one cigar at a time.

There is nothing difficult about giving up
smoking — I've done it hundreds of times
myself.

I have been reading the morning paper.
I do it every morning — well knowing that I
shall find in it the usual depravities and
baseness and hypocrisies and cruelties
that make up civilization, and cause me to
put in the rest of the day pleading for the
damnation of the human race.

If man could be crossed with the cat it would
improve man, but it would deteriorate the cat.

The human race consists of the
dangerously insane and such as are not.

Noise proves nothing. Often a hen who has merely laid an egg cackles as if she had laid an asteroid.

As out of place as a Presbyterian in Hell.

"Fortune knocks at every man's door once in a life," but in a good many cases the man is in a neighboring saloon and does not hear her.

I do not like work even when someone else does it.

When I was a boy of fourteen, my father was so ignorant I could hardly stand to have the old man around. But when I got to be twenty-one, I was astonished at how much he had learned in seven years.

ON WAR

There never was a just one, never an honorable one — on the part of the instigator of the war. I can see a million years ahead, and this rule will never change in so many as half a dozen instances.
The loud little handful — as usual — will shout for the war. The pulpit will object at first, the great dull bulk of the nation will rub its sleepy eyes and try to make out why there should be a war and will say earnestly and indignantly, "It is unjust and dishonorable and there is no necessity for it." Then the handful will shout louder. A few fair men on the other side will argue and reason against the war with speech and pen, and at first will have a hearing and be applauded; but it will not last long; those others will outshout them, and presently the anti-war audiences will thin out and lose popularity.

Before long you will see this curious thing:
the speakers stoned from the platform and
free speech strangled by hordes of furious
men who in their secret hearts are still at one
with those stoned speakers . . . but do not
dare to say so. And now the whole nation —
pulpit and all — will take up the war-cry
and shout itself hoarse, and mob any honest
man who ventures to open his mouth; and
presently such mouths will cease to open.
Next the statesmen will invent cheap lies
putting the blame upon the nation that is
attacked; and every man will be glad of those
conscience-soothing falsities, and will
diligently study them and refuse to examine
any refutations of them; and thus he will
by and by convince himself that the war is
just and will thank God for the better sleep
he enjoys after this process of
grotesque self-deception.

Persons attempting to find a motive in this narrative will be prosecuted; persons attempting to find a moral in it will be banished; persons attempting to find a plot in it will be shot. (Adventures of Huckleberry Finn.)

An Englishman is a person who does things because they have been done before.
An American is a person who does things because they haven't been done before.

An Irishman is lined with copper, and the beer corrodes it. But whiskey polishes the copper and is the saving of him.

Whenever the literary German dives into a sentence, that is the last you are going to see of him till he emerges on the other side of the Atlantic with his verb in his mouth.

Everybody talks about the weather
but nobody does anything about it.

I believe that our Heavenly Father invented
man because he was disappointed in the
monkey.

If Christ were here now there is one thing he would not be — a Christian.

My advice to girls:
first, don't smoke — to excess;
second, don't drink — to excess;
third, don't marry — to excess.

If you can't get a compliment any other way, pay yourself one.

If you tell the truth you don't have to remember anything.

The best way to cheer yourself up
is to try to cheer somebody else up.

It is a mistake that there is no bath that will cure people's manners, but drowning would help.

The man with a new idea is a crank until the idea succeeds.

It is not best that we should all think alike; it is difference of opinion that makes horse races.

It is easier to stay than get out.

Vast material prosperity always brings in its train conditions which debase the morals and enervate the manhood of a nation.

Loyalty to petrified opinion never yet
broke a chain or freed a human soul.

**There are several good protections against
temptations, but the surest is cowardice.**

Courage is resistance to fear, mastery of fear,
— not absence of fear.

My conscience is more trouble and bother
to me than anything else I started with.

It could probably be shown by facts and figures that there is no distinctly native American criminal class except Congress.

In statesmanship get the formalities right, never mind about the moralities.

All you need in this life is ignorance
and confidence, and then Success is sure.

**Put all your eggs in one basket and —
WATCH THAT BASKET.**

There is an old-time toast which is golden
for its beauty. "When you ascend the hill of
prosperity may you not meet a friend."

Good breeding consists in concealing how much we think of ourselves and how little we think of the other person.

You aim for the palace and get drowned in the sewer.

Let us be thankful for the fools. But for them the rest of us could not succeed.

The holy passion of Friendship is of so sweet and steady and loyal and enduring a nature that it will last through a whole lifetime — if not asked to lend money.

If there was an all-powerful God, he would have made all good, and no bad.

Whoever has lived long enough to find out what life is, knows how deep a debt of gratitude we owe to Adam, the first great benefactor of our race. He brought death into the world.

Most people are bothered by those passages of Scripture they do not understand, but the passages that bother me are those I do understand.

All you need in this life is ignorance
and confidence, and then Success is sure.

**Put all your eggs in one basket and —
WATCH THAT BASKET.**

There is an old-time toast which is golden
for its beauty. "When you ascend the hill of
prosperity may you not meet a friend."

It could probably be shown by facts and figures that there is no distinctly native American criminal class except Congress.

In statesmanship get the formalities right, never mind about the moralities.

You can't pray a lie.

Tomorrow night I appear for the first time
before a Boston audience — 4000 critics.

The reports of my death are greatly
exaggerated.

Nothing so needs reforming as other people's habits.

A baby is an inestimable blessing and bother.

Always do right. This will gratify some people, and astonish the rest.

The duel is one of the most dangerous institutions; since it is always fought in the open at daybreak, the combatants are sure to catch cold.

We should be careful to get out of an
experience only the wisdom that is in it. . . .
The cat that sits down on a hot stove lid will
never sit down on a hot stove lid again —
and that is well; but also she will never
sit down on a cold one any more.

Everyone is a moon, and has a dark side
which he never shows to anybody.

**Do something every day that you don't
want to do; this is the golden rule for
acquiring the habit of doing your duty
without pain.**

Columbus elaborated a deep plan to find a new route to an old country. Circumstance revised his plan for him, and he found a new *world*. And *he* gets the credit of it to this day. He hadn't anything to do with it.

My kind of loyalty was loyalty to one's
country, not to its institutions or its
officeholders. The country is the real thing,
the substantial thing, the eternal thing;
it is the thing to watch over, and care for,
and be loyal to.

**Almost any man worth his salt would fight
to defend his home, but no one ever heard
of a man going to war for his boarding house.**

Among the three or four million cradles now
rocking in the land are some which this nation
would preserve for ages as sacred things,
if we could know which ones they are.

There is no other life; life itself is only a vision and a dream, for nothing exists but space and you.

Death, the only immortal who treats us all
alike, whose pity and whose peace and whose
refuge are for all — the soiled and the pure,
the rich and the poor, the loved and
the unloved.
— Memorandum written on his deathbed